101

SERIOUS
MONEY
SELLING
TIPS

By Matt Oechsli

Other books by Matt Oechsli:

FastTrack Coaching
How to Build a 21st Century Financial Practice
The Intangibles Process
Winning the Inner Game of Selling
101 Tips for Coaching Financial Advisors
101 Tips for Becoming a Preferred Wholesaler

Printed in the United States of America.

ISBN: 0-9656765-2-8

Book design and cover graphics by Kerri Lindley

For more information about Matt Oechsli or
The Oechsli Institute, please visit our website at:
www.oechsli.com or call 800-883-6582

Total Achievement Publishing
PO Box 29385
Greensboro, NC 27429

It's a known fact that a single idea, received at the right time by an inquisitive and open mind, has the potential to propel that individual beyond their comfort zone into endeavors they had not thought possible. Whether it comes in the form of a solution or a brand new opportunity, the "that's what I need to do" reality that emerges from a simple idea can be powerful indeed.

Here are 101 such ideas, dedicated to providing breakthroughs in Serious Money Selling that will enable you to soar to new heights in the 21st century.

1

The upper middle-class and affluent do not want a sales person advising them on their serious financial affairs.

2

The upper-middle class and affluent need to be sold on your ability to solve their problems.

3

As a financial professional in the 21st century, your sales skills must be so refined, so well crafted, so practiced that they appear seamless to your affluent prospects.

4

You must be fully aware that you and every member of your team, group, or practice are the product that you are selling.

5

You must clearly define the profile of the ideal client you want to attract, service, and retain. You cannot target the affluent while still trying to be all things to everyone.

6

It's your ability to listen that enables you to sense areas of dissatisfaction, detect opportunities to take the next step, and recognize buying signals that beg the next mini-close. You need to be listening 80% of the time.

7

Face-to-face is basic for selling your services to the affluent. It activates a natural process that allows them to know you and determine whether or not they like you. Affluent prospects will only allow you to compete for their serious money if they discover reasons to like you.

8

You will make your first impression within the first three minutes, possibly in the first 30 seconds. This initial impression can ultimately make or break the sale.

9

Selling by telling will produce results you won't want to talk about.

10

In your efforts to attract affluent clients, remember that one face-to-face contact with a qualified prospect or center of influence is the equivalent of 300 cold calls of yesteryear.

11

Serious money selling is serious business. It requires a 7-day, every waking hour mind-set. Real financial pros are always prepared when they encounter, face-to-face, a potential prospect – whether by design or by accident.

12

Your ability to articulate true value, without sounding like a walking talking cliché, is essential. Trust must be established before you can achieve professional respect.

13

In the 21st century world of financial services, if you lead by proposing a product rather than a solution, you will be perceived as a sales person. To propose a solution, you must first understand the problem.

14

Learn to probe problems and articulate solutions that sound natural in the course of a normal conversation.

15

Describing financial services in terms of protection and growth options enables you to sell concepts, processes, and solutions rather than products.

16

You must make it more comfortable for a qualified prospect to accept your mini-close than it would be for them to say "no thanks."

17

A fancy brochure is often perceived as a sales piece by affluent prospects. Your collateral materials should articulate who you are, how your financial advisory process works, and the benefits of doing business with you.

18

Willie Sutton was once asked, "Why do you rob banks?" He replied, "That's where the money is!" To succeed in the world of serious money you too must go where the money is…

- **Generators of Wealth**: entrepreneurs, small business owners, partners in professional practices
- **Earners of Wealth**: executives, upper management, and highly paid sales people.
- **Receivers of Wealth**: inheritance, divorce settlements, insurance claims, or retirement.
- **Managers of Wealth**: human resource managers, municipalities, or union representatives.

Go, therefore, and find!

19

You must be able to recognize financial impact points during the course of a casual conversation. Any mention of anxiety, misunderstanding, or questions relating to money are great door openers to a future face-to-face meeting.

20

When recommending a financial solution, use a story to illustrate how it benefited another client. Stories create an "aha" response, enabling you to connect on an emotional level.

21

Build a library of success stories that can be used to illustrate how you can apply the right solutions to a variety of financial problems. The skill is in using a given story to make the appropriate emotional and rational impact.

22

It is also valuable to have a library of *tragic consequences* stories to be used whenever a qualified prospect is resisting or procrastinating. In the world of insurance, this is known as "Backing the hearse up to the kitchen door."

23

When face-to-face, your first objective is to establish rapport. Asking general questions about them, their family, and their interests will build rapport faster than anything you tell them about yourself.

24

Once you have established rapport, you can begin asking more penetrating questions about their financial affairs. However, it's important to ask permission before doing so.

25

Receiving permission to ask penetrating questions about a prospect's financial and personal affairs brings with it an implied receptiveness to your next mini-close.

26

When a prospect hesitates to answer a question, it's wise to assume that sufficient rapport has not yet been established. Back off and simply continue on a friendly conversation level.

27

Attention to detail, whether it's follow-up phone calls, meeting deadlines, remembering names, or simply doing the little things right, adds up to provide the tangible evidence that you will be a dependable "go-to" advisor.

28

It is not enough to under-stand and believe in the financial services that you offer. You must also be convinced that others need those services and it's your calling to convince them of that fact.

29

You must apply your sales skills every working day. This keeps you sharp, strengthens your focus, and uncovers opportunities that you would otherwise miss.

30

A real pro never hires a junior person to do his or her serious money selling.

31

You can hire a financial planner, a CPA, an attorney, or any other professional. But you cannot hire someone else to be your "rainmaker."

32

You must be able to offer clear financial solutions to clients and qualified prospects at the drop of a hat, with both ease and consistency.

33

Your daily sales and relationship building efforts mirror your internal goal commitment.

34

In order to successfully attract, service and retain affluent clients in the 21st century, your short-term goals and daily activities need to be directly linked to your long-range business plan.

35

You cannot successfully target upper-middle class and affluent prospects while continuing to open small accounts. The selling effort and service needs are different, and those needs will continually be in conflict.

36

Selling is still a numbers game, but today, you need to focus on the numbers that define your "ideal" client.

- What is the minimum level of investable assets that you will accept?
- How many current clients meet your Ideal Client Profile?
- How many current clients can you upgrade to ideal within the next 12 months?
- How many people do you know that can introduce you to individuals who match your Ideal Client Profile?

That shift in focus will reduce your number of clients while increasing your assets and production.

37

Selling financial solutions to the affluent is more complex, and that means a longer sales cycle. Sales activity, needs to be tracked on a weekly, monthly, and quarterly basis. A true pro always knows where he or she stands relative to achieving annual goals.

38

Activity drives the dream. You must identify and track the number of daily contacts required to produce the weekly face-to-face appointments necessary to meet your monthly and quarterly targets.

39

High level selling requires discipline, both in planning and in doing what needs to be done. Devote a couple hours of your Sunday afternoon to plan your upcoming week, and spend 30 minutes at the end of each day to review what you accomplished and plan the upcoming day.

40

Some of your prospects will be direct, outspoken, and impatient. Others will be talkative, enthusiastic, and optimistic. Still others will be more easygoing, warm, and friendly. And there will be those who are more distant, reserved, and restrained. Communicating effectively with each of these behavioral styles is essential to high-level sales success. Adapt your communication style to meet the style needs of each prospect.

41

A strong ego and thick skin are important qualities for success in selling. When dealing with the upper-middle class and affluent, it's important to balance these qualities with sincere empathy and caring.

42

A true pro never attempts to fake sincerity.

43

You cannot afford to take rejection personally. Use it for motivation. Allow it to be a learning experience that enables you to refine your skills. Never let it get you down for longer than 10 seconds. Then ask for a referral.

44

Many people delay making decisions, where serious money is concerned. Shorten that delay by carefully helping clients and prospects find reasons for being dissatisfied with their status quo. If you can offer a solution that transforms their dissatisfaction into a sense of urgency, they will quickly decide in your favor.

45

Your most important sale is to yourself. You must be so convinced of the value you provide and the quality of the processes you use to deliver that value, that you are willing to talk with every individual who has, or can connect you with, serious money.

46

The more a financial professional loves selling in the serious money arena, the greater number of face-to-face contacts they will make, the more refined and seamless their skills will become, and the greater their success will be.

47

Dressing for success takes on a different "look" in the world of serious money. Real pros are not flashy. They are attired in business suits that project consummate professionalism. Dark blue inspires trust; casual attire is out and so is excessive jewelry. Everything counts.

48

Whenever in doubt regarding your attire for a social event, dress one level up. Remember that you are always on stage, whether you're at a picnic, ball game, or the opera.

49

Social prospecting is an essential skill for successfully selling financial services to the affluent. Most of their serious decisions are made because of word-of-mouth influence.

50

A well-trained financial professional always recognizes connecting opportunities, whether they are in social settings, casual encounters, or official appointments. The pro is always prepared to smoothly switch from social to business related conversation.

51

Closing opportunities are only valuable to financial professionals who recognize the buying signals and capitalize on the opportunity presented. It's all about being able to close the deal on cue.

52

55% of buying signals come in the form of nonverbal gestures. Observing body language will tell you when a prospect is ready to hear your proposal – or when you are <u>not</u> connecting.

53

Yes, you do have to close the sale. Studies show that 50% of financial professionals forget to ask for the business. Another 35% will ask for the business, but accept whatever excuse is given, and never ask again. The most successful use mini-closes to continue the closing process until the relationship is consummated.

54

Ask a trusted colleague to point out your strengths and weaknesses. Nothing is more debilitating than a blind spot that continually sabotages your best intentions.

55

Often your first mini-close will be asking for and getting that first face-to-face meeting with an affluent prospect.

56

Scheduling a follow-up meeting with a qualified prospect should take the form of a mini-close. That meeting will be far more productive if your prospect will agree to complete specific tasks before you meet again.

57

The ability to gain professional respect is critical. It
requires communication
skills, a defined Financial
Advisory Process, and the
resolve to deliver on all
promises.

58

Trust is essential in the world of serious money. It is continually redefined through every form of contact, communication, and action taken. Every time you exaggerate, over-promise, over-flatter, or trash your competition, you plant a seed of distrust.

59

Major decisions are made when there is harmony between the emotional and rational dimensions of the buying decision making process.

60

If you overload a prospect
with too much information,
it can cause indecision and
procrastination.

61

If a prospect asks about fees, resist the temptation to answer directly unless they are already sold on doing business with you. Explain that it is impossible to discuss fees without a clear understanding of their needs.

62

You must have a mini-presentation (one or two brief sentences) ready whenever the opportunity is presented. Whether in an elevator (hence the term 'elevator speech') or in a coffee shop, windows of opportunity with serious money will occur if you are ready.

63

Adding value by providing the unexpected has become common practice when working with the affluent. What used to be considered a competitive advantage must now become a regular part of your modus operandi.

64

Skill in asking financially specific *what, where, when, why* and *who* questions is an essential part of probing into the story behind the financial impact points that you uncover.

65

Assisting a select group of families with their complex financial affairs is challenging, but it is far more powerful than being one-dimensional and only handling your clients' investments.

66

Be careful how you de-scribe your practice. You must always be what you say you are.

67

Uncovering and creating dissatisfaction during casual conversation with an affluent prospect is an essential component of social prospecting.

68

Anticipate common objections and you will be prepared for them. Overcoming objections is a natural part of the sales cycle.

69

Asking for high quality referrals and introductions from key clients, centers-of-influence, and other professionals is rarely perceived as tacky or cheap. If clients value what you offer, they will recommend you to friends and colleagues.

70

Thanking a client or center-of-influence for a quality introduction is merely good manners. Presenting a small gift (movie tickets, lunch coupon, bottle of wine, etc.) is a nice touch, but resist being lavish.

71

The psychology of selling intangibles builds off dissatisfaction. Successful financial professionals are always looking for current events and personal experiences that cause concern for their clients and prospects.

72

Consistently updating your list of qualified prospects is the only way to stay current in your prospecting activities.

73

You must have a nose for money: new money, old money, money in motion, and distress money. Smelling that money should make you eager to get face-to-face with a serious money decision maker.

74

To ensure that prospecting occurs in a disciplined manner, you must have a *prospecting system* that is a high priority. Prospecting for serious money is an every day activity!

75

Being able to quickly qualify and confirm a prospect's potential is essential. Nothing wastes more time than romancing an unqualified prospect.

76

Keep a Referral Notebook with the name of a "Top Client" at the top of each page. Underneath, list the names of individuals they mention during business and casual conversations. Later, call your client back and ask to be introduced or referred to one of the people listed under their name.

77

Whenever you receive a referral, make contact within 24 hours. Always use the name of the person who referred you. Assure them that this is not a sales call, but that you simply would like to make his or her acquaintance over a cup of coffee (or something equally innocent).

78

Keeping track of your pipeline is as important as keeping your qualified prospect list current. At all times, you must know the number of prospects, the potential assets they represent, and where they are in their buying decision process.

79

In terms of having emotional impact, there is nothing as powerful as a smile. A genuine smile not only makes us feel good, it makes those around us feel good.

80

It's true that people tend to react positively to a genuine smile of enjoyment. But beware of the false overly toothy smile that is associated with insincerity.

81

Projecting relaxed confidence to a qualified prospect naturally transfers positive energy. This is why pros turn qualified prospects into ideal clients faster than most.

82

You need to understand the buying decision making process of each prospect and then walk in step with them. Being in step enables you to know exactly where they are and sense how to keep pulling them along.

83

Research tells us that affluent investors are searching for a "go-to" trustworthy financial professional who is unbiased, a good problem solver, and can oversee a wide range of financial protection, investment, disbursement, and philanthropic needs.

84

Because the solutions you are selling provide for a broad range of financial needs, you must have clarity in your organization about who does what, how and why. There must be high efficiency and no ambiguity.

85

Most affluent prospects have more than one individual giving them financial advice. However, they would prefer to have one trusted financial quarterback who can pull all the disparate financial pieces together. Work to become that "go-to" advisor, one client at a time.

86

With distrust being so prevalent within the financial services industry, every affluent prospect is on the alert for any form of incongruence. Pay attention to every statement, mannerism, promise, and follow-up action, and you will transform this negative expectation into a strong bond of trust.

87

Take nothing about serious money sales for granted. Recite your lines, role-play, script how you will overcome objections, practice your mini-closes, and craft a number of closes that you can adapt to any opportunity.

88

You strengthen your relationships on a visceral level by making each ideal prospect feel as though he or she is the only person on your calendar, that time is irrelevant, and that you are totally at their disposal.

89

Using carefully crafted questions, allows you to guide the conversation away from yourself and into the realm of your prospects' interests. The more they talk, the more you learn, and the better they will like you.

90

Remember that an individual's name is to that person the sweetest and most important sound in any language. Memorize it quickly and use it often, but always in a natural and conversational way.

91

Whenever you are unsure of a prospect's answer to one of your questions, ask for clarification. It is always better to ask than to assume, only to find out that you were wrong. Asking shows that you care.

92

Mirroring body language, speech pattern, and voice level enhances rapport. If your prospect stands, you stand. If they speak slowly and deliberately, you slow down to their pace. This keeps communication at an adult-to-adult level.

93

Whenever you are attacked, personally or professionally, never argue. But, do not turn the other cheek completely. Let the attack finish, maintaining constant eye contact. Control your breathing, and then counter with a relaxed and professional comeback. You are a professional, and you do not tolerate bad manners. Good clients have evolved from taking this approach. It's like standing up to a bully.

94

Always be on time whether for a casual get-together, an official appointment, a social engagement, or a follow-up telephone call. Being on time tells them they are important to you.

95

The little things you continually do add value. That's why they mean a lot.

96

The broader your interests and breadth of knowledge in areas outside the world of financial services, the greater opportunity you will have to build rapport and benefit from social networking with the affluent.

97

Do not attempt to impress an affluent prospect by using financial industry jargon. It's a turn-off. Practice speaking in a language they can easily understand, regardless of how complex the financial topic.

98

Represent yourself accurately at all times. Honesty is the only policy. Until they realize they can fully trust you, the affluent will be looking for any form of disconnect.

99

Be humble.

100

Avoid mechanical and contrived contacts. Form letters, unsigned birthday cards, and ghostwritten newsletters all ring hollow in the mind of the affluent.

101

Schedule child focused outings for the entire family of your top clients. With a little creativity, picnics, petting zoos, carnivals, etc. can become events children remember. If they remember, you profit.

Bonus Tip

High achieving financial
professionals constantly
look for ways to motivate
themselves.

Bonus Tip

High achieving financial professionals think big. Most people don't because they are afraid to fail.

THE OECHSLI INSTITUTE

- AV Presentations
- Research Reports
- Books
- Business Development KITS
- Individual & Team Assessment
- Coaching Support
- Speaking & Training

---

www.oechsli.com
800-883-6582